Love Made Real

Poetic Reflections on the Love, Life, and Light of Christ

Gloria Yoder Ewachiw

Love Made Real

Poetic Reflections on the Love, Light, and Life of Christ

by
Gloria Yoder Ewachiw

Compiler: Bonnie Frick

ISBN-13: 978-1978439764
ISBN-10: 1978439768

Printed in the United States of America
by
CreateSpace, an Amazon.com Company

Available from Amazon.com and other retail outlets.

**Dedicated to the loving memory of my mother,
Eva Elston Yoder**

My husband accepted a new job, causing our family to move from Pennsylvania to Michigan. His need to leave a month ahead of the children and me left me with preparing my beloved "dream home" for sale. Every day, my dear, heartbroken mother came to help me. Occasionally, friends stopped by to say goodbye, sometimes bringing farewell gifts. On one such occasion, after a friend had left, Mother sadly shared that everyone was giving me such lovely gifts and that all she had to give me was "this dirty apron."

A DIRTY APRON

Many gifts have come to me
but, looking back, I only see–

a dirty apron.

A garment worn with humble air
and, yet, with grace so truly rare–

that dirty apron.

No measure there
of help and care,
of anguish shared
and burden spared;
of loving pride
held tight inside
and sacrificed
with heavy price.

The world would benefit if more
would wear the way my mother wore

a dirty apron.

Acknowledgements

It's been said that "writing is fun, but publishing is hard work". Because of my limitations regarding such, I have been a bit overwhelmed by friends who not only encouraged me but volunteered assistance in making this little booklet possible. My deepest appreciation would be insufficient to express my feelings about the help they have rendered.

First, Willow Valley's Chaplain Kenneth Phillips, who recommended the undertaking, was largely responsible for putting the whole procedure into motion. I am so grateful for his caring interest, leadership, computer skills, creativity, and his untiring guidance – the list goes on and on.

When my friend and fellow resident, Mrs. Bonnie Frick, heard of the venture, she immediately offered her teacher's writing and organizational skills, and spent many long hours developing a draft for Chaplain Phillips to employ. She puts a new "happy face" on friendship.

Thank you both so much!

Table of Contents

Thoughts 9

God and Son 15

Birth 27

Death and Resurrection 39

Love 55

Life 67

Light 77

Eternity 83

Thoughts

APPLE WISDOM

As I sliced into the apple,
the thought occurred to me–
there's something more to this
than what the eye can see.

A single, simple piece of fruit,
oft blamed for mankind's woes,
now appeared before me
as lovely as a rose.

My thoughts were lifted higher
by an offbeat symmetry
that suddenly transformed it
into the Holy Trinity.

The skin's surrounding protection
represents God's love and worth;
the flesh inside resembles
the life of Christ on earth.

Leaving buried deep inside it
the seeds for reproduction–
the means of growth and guidance
through the Holy Spirit's instruction.

I will never look at an apple again
without musing over these facts–
realizing what it means to my spirit
and praising the power it packs!

A CHILD AGAIN

When the world presses in close about me
and I am by its pleasures beguiled;
when the things in my life threaten triumph,
Lord, give me the *FAITH* of a child.

When my eyes grow dim to life's beauty
and my sense of wonder's defiled,
bring me back to a sense of adventure.
Lord, give me the *JOY* of a child.

If I no longer find time for searching
and my wisdom is wholly self-styled,
make me thirsty again for your teachings.
Lord, give me the *MIND* of a child.

When doubts creep into my thinking
and hope becomes dismally mild;
when anxiety rules daily living,
Lord, give me the *TRUST* of a child.

When unhappiness leaves me unfeeling
for fate no longer has smiled,
turn my self-interest back into caring.
Lord, give me the *HEART* of a child

If I'm tempted to dwell on an island
for with people I'm easily riled,
remind me that Christ died for all men.
Lord, give me the *LOVE* of a child.

SEASONED OBSERVATION

Nature sends Summer in alluring array;
we're lulled by the music–she dances away.

Autumn stalks in with its dazzle instead,
stating emphatically, "Summer is dead!"

Soon Winter blitzes and blusters about,
stripping the splendor that gave Autumn clout.

But the Ruler of Nature proves once more He's King:
He has the final word–we call it Spring!

LIFE GOES ON

That dark bare tree
stands bravely there
as winter winds deploy.
Once, clothed in brilliance,
it had a life
of beauty and of joy.
However, this
is not the end,
for naught can e'er destroy
its vibrant color.
'Twill soon return–
our faithful God's envoy.

ENCOURAGEMENT

When you're feeling down,
keep looking up!
When it's nearly empty,
God will fill your cup.

When your faith seems fragile
and your hope grows dim,
remember Jesus loves you–
keep on trusting Him.

When your craft hits rough water
and the going gets tough
and you feel as though
you've had more than enough–

Trust in your Captain
to see you through.
He's watching and waiting
to hear from you.

God and Son

HOW DO YOU PICTURE GOD?

So many people picture God
as a very aged man.
In their finite minds they see–
a tired "also ran."

He doesn't really understand
our needs regarding life and such.
Although "advanced" in terms of years,
He seems completely out of touch.

Why should they trust in such a God
drawn from ancient history,
when all they've ever known of Him
is shrouded in such mystery?

They simply just don't get it–
God completely transcends time.
No matter what our age might be,
He is always in His prime.

Because we have our limits, we
can't think beyond the box.
God's not confined to "past" or "future,"
"He **IS**" – forget your clocks!

Because He really loves us,
He reached out a powerful hand
and sent His Son to prove it
as He had always planned.

How can anyone ignore that love?
How can any turn aside?
God **IS** the Ruler of all Time
and wants to be our Guide.

We need to say, "I do accept
the gift of your dear Son,"
and time will no more rule our lives–
God **IS** the only One!

17

GOD IS A MYSTERY

God is a mystery for us indeed;
we can't understand or explain
the power behind that holy throne,
but our loss becomes our gain.

Our sin caused a great gulf between us,
but our God created a way–
He bridged that gap with the love of Christ
and strengthened our feet of clay.

For He sent forth the Holy Spirit
to comfort and guide us each day,
whose presence is there for the asking
with faith and trust leading the way.

It doesn't sound like an easy endeavor
to trust what we can't understand.
That's true, but it really is worth it–
just reach out for the Father's Hand.

Yes, the power of God is a mystery–
a mystery we treasure and trust,
and in the love of God we're rejoicing,
for we know His purpose is just.

REALITY

Each day it seems
I read or hear what
foolishness is found in faith;
it is not logical nor scientific
nor can one offer proof.

A "figment of imagination",
the "opiate of masses",
a cruel tool of devious minds
designed to enslave the innocent

But they have never met my Jesus!

He simply cannot be
explained away and,
in the deepest regions of
my heart and soul,
His Spirit dwells and
whispers

I AM REALITY

SILENCE

Do not fear the silence–
it is a friend–
a friend with whom you
share your joy and daily
pain.

Wear it as a cloak and
draw its richness
close about you.

Spread it wide and
feel it billow
with the breeze of Life.

Know it as
the habitation of your
God–
He dwells in Silence.

FAMILY OF GOD

Family life is truly a blessing,
and being loved is a vital need.
God understands more than we do,
for it was He who planted the seed.

We can't choose our earthly family,
and God realizes that as well.
Family life is not always perfect,
but our fears He will gladly quell.

He has made us a better offer
than we could hope to attain,
adopting us as sons and daughters
and turning our losses to gain.

We just need to reach out in faith
and believe in His own dear Son.
Our Father in Heaven will welcome us all.
With the Family of God, we are one!

THE SEA OF FAITH

Our Heavenly Father's
tempting gift of love,
the sea of faith, is like unto
the oceans that surround us–
a vast expanse
with few embracing it in
quite the same way.

Some take the plunge and
plumb the depths without a doubt,
diving underneath some waves that later
crash upon the shore.

Others slowly tiptoe in,
testing carefully the temperature and depth
in an effort to avoid
the ever-constant
force of undertow
determined to control the flow of faith
in daily living.

So natured, they may never know
the strength and beauty that is
ever-present in the God
they claim to trust,
and may forever spend their time
just wandering on the
fringes of faith.

GOD IS

The message of God in Christ

is trampled

    distorted

      exploited

        drowned out in the deafening din

created by a mindless marathon:

  ritualized tradition,

  tin-pan alley trappings of emotionalism,

  purely intellectual pursuit of theological theory,

  super-saturation of social gratification,

  careless immaturity of misguided idealism.

Wherever men are willing to forego:

  pleasure of projecting their thoughts, wills, and voices,

  satisfaction of having all the answers,

  security of confining God to paper–

the **GOOD NEWS**

      stands out in bas relief

      with power, love and hope.

In the spine-tingling terror of time–

      GOD IS!

RIVER RUNNER

Though the vessel was small and the cargo light,
the course was true and the course was right;
and it mattered not whether day or night–
he steered it well–yes, he steered it well.

When morning broke and the day'd begin
and the sun rose warm as his lovely grin,
he would cruise the shore where he'd often been–
and he steered it well–ah, he steered it well.

He held to the code as he held the wheel,
for he knew the rules and the rules were real;
and they kept his craft on an even keel
as he steered it well–how he steered it well!

If the day were dark and the going rough
and the way were grim and the way were tough;
when other vessels had had enough,
he steered it well–true, he steered it well.

When the mooring was reached and the anchor cast,
the voyage was ended; the voyage past.
He turned to his SKIPPER–safe at last,
for he'd steered it well–aye, he'd steered it well!

WHAT GOD CANNOT DO

God cannot be tempted by evil,
nor can He be labeled unjust.
He cannot break any promises
and cannot betray our trust.

He cannot tell lies; He is the Truth.
He cannot force anyone to love Him,
nor can He abandon His children,
For He cannot succumb to a whim.

I'm certain there are other "cannots."
But here's what makes life brand new–
He cannot envision our sins at all
since Jesus' blood blocks them from view.

PART-TIME SAVIOR

There's no such thing as a part-time Savior–
Jesus is a full-time Lord.
When life is good, we think we don't need Him,
and with His message we're bored.
But picking and choosing is not an option
to serve the One we've adored.
It's all or nothing where He is concerned–
anything less, we cannot afford.

YEAST

We're called to be the yeast that makes
    God's Holy Kingdom grow.

What once was just unleavened bread
    takes on a greater glow.

Yeast is such a simple force,
    but it works–however slow.

Small beginnings yield great gain
    and so is yeast applied.

Though its presence may not be seen,
    its strength can't be denied.

Our task? To share just one-on-one
    with Jesus as our guide,

His love, His life, His Kingdom, too,
    in which we take such pride.

Jesus is the Bread of Life,
    and His feast will long abide.

Birth

ISAIAH

The Lord God needed a messenger;
and Isaiah thus had a vision
where all his sins were burned away,
and he made a landmark decision.

He would share God's promise with the people
in spite of their penchant for sinning.
A great light would shine in the darkness
and offer a brand new beginning.

DAVID

Just a simple shepherd boy, Jesse's youngest son,
fought the giant Goliath and that battle WON!

Later, God anointed him to wear the royal crown
and as King of Israel was held in great renown.

Through tragedies and triumphs, he led the nation on,
even though, at times, it did appear all hope was gone.

God had made specific plans in his Divine Design;
the Messiah thus descended from David's royal line.

ZECHARIAH

Zechariah was performing priestly duty
in the Temple when Gabriel appeared,
announcing the birth of a son to his wife–
a message from God that seemed weird.

Zechariah simply could not believe it,
for he and his wife were quite old;
so Gabriel declared him unable to speak
until the promised birth would unfold.

When the prophesied baby boy arrived,
Zechariah wrote down his choice.
"His name must be John," as Gabriel decreed;
then Zechariah regained his voice.

JOHN THE BAPTIST

John the Baptist was truly unique.
His mission: prepare to loudly proclaim
the coming of Jesus, God's only Son,
after which life would ne'er be the same.

John preached and baptized the people,
urging repentance, new life, and thus.
John introduced the Messiah
who proved God loves all of us.

NAZARETH GRAPEVINE

The grapevine was humming
    and grim news quickly spread.
Young Mary was expecting,
    and though betrothed–not wed!

It circulated round her friends
    with the power to amaze.
They adored her gentle spirit
    and her kind and caring ways.

It was hard for them to fathom,
    for she was a proven devout Jew;
but other folks in Nazareth
    took a dim and different view.

They would scorn what they knew not
    and cause Mary great pain.
She bore her burden bravely;
    in her heart 'twas not in vain.

It must have been so difficult–
    she didn't really understand
what was happening in her young life,
    but God's wish was her command.

And, as His handmaid, she embraced
    what lay ahead with trust;
to face the future unafraid,
    accepting God's will as just.

Regarding Nazareth's old grapevine–
    its members have long passed away.
But, as those who've met Mary's Son know,
    her example of faith's here to stay.

JOSEPH'S OBEDIENCE

Joseph was engaged to Mary, whom he loved,
but he received some shattering news–
she was expecting a child that was not his.
It was a message designed to confuse.

He decided to break up privately,
not wanting to see her disgraced.
It was surely the hardest decision
that he ever before had faced.

Then God's angel appeared in a dream,
advising him to make Mary his wife.
The Child, conceived by God's Spirit,
would be named Jesus and change all of life.

AN INNKEEPER'S DILEMMA

He was a very busy fellow–
   what a harried life he led!
So many census travelers
   were needing food and bed.

Bethlehem was overflowing
   with strangers and their kin,
and no matter how he scuffled
   it seemed he couldn't win.

Tempers flared around him;
   he was weary from demands.
He kept reminding people
   that he only had two hands.

So when the "hand of history"
   came knocking at his door,
it was just another peasant
   who'd be wanting even more.

Well, he had his answer ready,
   and poor Joseph bore the brunt.
"There is no room available!"
   His statement was quite blunt.

But perhaps his wife noticed Mary
   who was surely great with child.
With Joseph looking frantic–
   she beckoned them and smiled.

That may be why a manger
   would hold the newborn King
whose coming from the Father
   made hosts of angels sing.

If that innkeeper had only witnessed
   the truth of the Christ Child's glory,
can you imagine his reaction
   if he knew "the rest of the story"?

MANGER MIRACLE!

A miracle took place in a manger!
The Son of God would thus arrive.
Till then, He was a virtual stranger,
but now "in the flesh" is alive.

In the midst of a census uproar,
a child quietly and humbly was born,
but very few noticed what happened
on that inconspicuous morn.

Just a simple wooden food trough–
yet from its common core arose
love such as man had never known
all wrapped in swaddling clothes.

The King of Kings born in a stable–
why a manger? What does it mean?
There must be a subtle reason
for our human hearts to glean.

Is it possible that humble beginning
that seems far beyond our ken
was intended to help us fathom
that Christ was sent for all men?

Now when we view that empty manger
it should give us "food for thought."
Unless we embrace God's miracle,
Christmas is all for naught!

THE APPEARANCE OF GOD

A star appeared,
followed by a singular birth.
A child appeared,
followed by life on this earth.
That life appeared
at a loving God's command.
The Messiah appeared
as God had always planned.

Jesus Christ appeared,
fulfilling God's true goals.
Salvation appeared
to a world of wounded souls.

A deadly cross appeared,
but through its pain and sorrow
a human choice appeared,
offering a bright tomorrow!

GROWING

He was born just a babe in a manger,
   clad only in swaddling cloths.
But He studied and grew into manhood,
   traveling the way of the Cross.

Our homage is not for the baby–
   whatever great beauty He holds.
We honor the Christ–risen Savior
   in whose life God's mercy unfolds.

So must we, rooted firmly in Jesus,
   leave our faith's early childhood behind.
As He grew both in wisdom and stature,
   so must we nourish heart, soul and mind.

Then when we are raised in His likeness,
   and Jesus lays claim to His own;
He will stand at the door–widely opened–
   saying, "Enter, my child, how you've grown."

GOD'S LIFELINE

From a bright star in the dark sky
to a stark cross on a hill–
symbols of a mission that
only God's Son could fulfill.

Today we glorify those signs
that marked our Savior's life,
but oft do forget His journey
was filled with pain and strife.

We see beauty in those symbols
in which we take such pride
but sometimes do gloss over.
They were intended as a guide.

The star has long since vanished
and the babe's no longer there;
the cross that bore our Father's love
is now completely bare.

Those symbols should direct our lives–
they happened for a reason;
and we must all remember that
for more than just a season.

Death and Resurrection

AMAZING JOURNEY

Bethlehem to Egypt,
Nazareth, and Galilee–
strange markers on the road
that led to Calvary.

A wondrous birth,
a quick escape,
quiet growing years–
a brief but potent ministry
led to a vale of tears.

A journey made by Jesus,
surrendering His will
to His Father's love for all mankind;
He struggled up that hill.

But His presence on Golgotha,
where three harsh crosses stood,
gives incredible new meaning
to the phrase, "Give once for good."

THE TRIUMPHANT ENTRY

"Hosanna!" cried the people
        when Jesus rode into view.
They'd heard so much about Him,
        and real excitement grew.

"Hosanna!" cried the people
        living under Roman rule.
They were hungry for deliverance
        from a life considered cruel.

"Hosanna!" cried the people
        as they spread palms in His path,
loudly singing and rejoicing,
        ignoring the enemy's wrath.

"Hosanna!" cried the people;
        loud hosannas they would sing.
If they had had a choice that hour,
        they would have crowned Him king!

But, then, just a few days later,
        there was heard a different cry
fueled by anger and disappointment–
        they would shout out, "Crucify!"

Jerusalem and Rome alike, you see
        found it hard to understand
the reason for the coming of Christ
        and the things that God had planned.

So as we all are shouting, "Hosanna!"
        at this Palm Sunday time
let us praise our Heavenly Father's
        great love and grace sublime.

THE LAST SUPPER

In a large and furnished Upper Room,
    they prepared to celebrate
the holy Feast of Passover
    with anticipation great.

But the meal they shared with Jesus
    was not what they expected;
and, at times, it was confusing–
    they felt puzzled and dejected.

First, when Jesus knelt before them
    with a basin to wash their feet,
they were stunned–their Master as a Servant?
    Crying, "No!" Peter leapt from his seat.

He tried to refuse the Lord's offer,
    but Jesus quietly rebuked him.
"If you don't allow me to serve you,
    our future together is dim."

Jesus spoke of betrayal and denial
    -and they knew He couldn't lie–
they voiced their fears and great concern,
    "Who is it, Lord? Is it I?"

Peter swore he'd never deny his Lord–
    he'd rather pay the ultimate price.
But Jesus responded with this prediction,
    "After three times the cock will crow twice."

Then Jesus turned to another disciple
    -for the issue was still a bit prickly–
He soberly spoke so Judas could hear,
    "What Thou doest, doest Thou quickly!"

When the Passover meal was finished,
    He held up a loaf of bread
representing His body to be broken
    and wine for the blood He would shed.

So, you see, the "last supper" became a first–
    lest anyone should ever forget,
Bread and wine to be shared "in remembrance"
    of the One who paid our great debt.

A CROSS. A CROOK. A CROWN.

Just three simple words
    filled with pain, love, and joy
paint a portrait of Jesus
    that man cannot destroy.

He endured the vile Cross
    and scorned all its shame,
knowing God would redeem Him,
    for He was not to blame.

We, too, must bear crosses–
    in life, we'll know pain
as Christ did before us–
    but our loss becomes gain.

As He rose from death's grasp,
    He assumed a new look–
changed from Victim to Shepherd,
    He bears now a Crook.

Though like sheep we wander,
    His great love will remain
to guide us and save us,
    for He died not in vain.

As Jesus challenged Peter,
    we, too, must feed His Sheep;
though the pathway grows narrow
    and the hills may be steep.

When the task is completed
        and His sheep have been fed,
He will lay down His Staff,
        and wear a Crown instead.

Then we who have loved Him
        will honor His Rod,
for He is the ruler of
        the Kingdom of God!

LOVE MADE REAL

Love is basically just a word
        lightly tossed around.

It comes in many shapes and forms
        which readily abound.

What makes the honest difference?
        When is love more than zeal

And not just a passing fancy
        with such limited appeal?

Only when our God the Lord
        who sent His only son,

Jesus, who gave for us His all,
        and was the only One

To demonstrate once and for all
        how we should feel.

In His Life and Cross we witness–
        love made real!

FEED MY SHEEP

Although Jesus had admonished Peter
    and urged caution regarding denial;
in spite of the Master's warning,
    Peter denied Him three times through the trial.

Imagine the pain that was Peter's
    when he heard the cock had crowed twice.
He realized he'd done what he ought not,
    while his master was paying a price.

But after the Resurrection, we're told,
    an interesting question arose–
"Do you love me?" Jesus asked Peter.
    This only added to Peter's woes.

Each time Peter answered, "Yes, Lord, I do."
    Jesus would reply, "Feed my sheep."
By the third time, Peter's feelings were hurt–
    Did the Lord think he'd been asleep?

Then the truth of the moment touched him;
    He realized what Jesus must mean.
When Jesus was gone, Peter would remain
    to command the earthly scene.

Aha, one question for each denial,
    and Peter knew the path must be trod;
he was forgiven and must spread the gospel
    to honor the Christ, Son of God.

PETER'S REBIRTH

I cannot believe what I'm hearing–
who in the world is that speaking?
Isn't he the one they call Peter
that authorities have been seeking?

Where has he been all this time?
Everyone knows he's a coward.
We all were so very certain
his faith in this Jesus had soured.

But who would expect him to boldly declare
in defense of the man who just died–
this Jesus who claimed that He was God
and whom our leaders had then crucified.

This same Peter asserts that God Himself
gave Jesus over to us to be killed–
but then God raised Him from the dead,
as He had so long before willed?

Doesn't he realize these statements of his
could cause great harm in his life?
This reckless courage that's pouring forth
might bring endless pain and strife.

Somehow, some way Peter had changed;
he had a totally different view.
He realized His Savior was truly alive;
thus, his old life became brand new.

THE VEIL

What was the purpose of the veil
that curtained the Holy Place?
What was closeted behind it
was a very privileged space.

Only the High Priest really knew,
and he just once in a year
could enter that hallowed ground
that for others held great fear.

A dwelling place for God Himself,
the "Holy of Holies" by name;
and on the hidden altar there
was laid all of Israel's blame.

But then something powerful happened–
a Jew claimed God loves everyone.
He owned that God was His Father,
and He was His only Son.

His enemies surrounded in anger,
demanding His claims be denied;
and, unfairly, He was nailed to a cross
where He suffered and bled and died.

That caused the earth to start quaking
as nature provided a clue–
the sky was darkened at midday,
and the veil was rent in two!

What really happened that day, you see,
old ways were left far behind–
God burst through the veil that divided
His mercy and love for mankind.

No more were sacrifices required–
that religious practice was diminished.
It happened that day on the rugged cross
when Jesus cried out, "It is finished!"

THE RESURRECTION

Mystery surrounds the Resurrection,
    and our finite minds fail to see
how Jesus escaped a stone-sealed tomb.
    Why did the Roman guards flee?

No one actually saw it happen–
    how do we know it's true?
An event that changed life forever
    was recorded by very few.

My heart goes out to poor Thomas
    with his honest, doubting ways.
Yet after he saw the wounds himself,
    his heart spilled over with praise.

How did His weary, disheartened followers
    know Jesus was snatched from death's jaws?
Why did their fears and doubts disappear
    when they gave their lives to His cause?

Knowledge has some powerful limits–
    and where faith cannot be explained,
it must be accepted with worship and trust
    and, thus, must our hearts be trained.

THE GOSSIP BENCH

You'll never believe what I just heard.
Remember all those noisy games
played by two kids here in our village?
Simon and John were their names.
Those boys were boisterous and rowdy;
and we certainly all did agree
they'd never amount to very much
once they left their mother's knee.

Well, we were right. Guess what I heard–
they both quit their jobs and left town.
Ah, their poor parents who wanted more
must really be feeling down.
Why would they do that? Well, it's said,
they followed some itinerant preacher–
who's made some incredible claims
and now wants to act as their teacher.
His name? I don't know. His father's Joseph–
a young upstart who was nothing more
than a carpenter's son–can you imagine?
And they haven't a clue what's in store!

(Time Passes)

Come here, everyone, I've got an update
on what happened to Simon and John.
Their "glorious leader" was arrested–
seems His teachings were frowned upon.
If they've any idea what will happen now,
they'll depart from Him in a hurry.
He's proved "nothing good comes from Nazareth."
If they're smart, they should start to worry.

By the way, that "glorious leader"
had the nerve to change Simon's name.
He called him Peter, the Rock, they said,
and he'll never again be the same.

(Time Passes)

What's that you say? There was a great crowd
gathered to hear Peter preaching–
claiming their dead master had risen,
and God was in charge of their teaching!
So many people believing a message
that Peter and John came to share–
absurd! They never knew those two.
How they must have changed–what a pair!
Perhaps we should go and listen
and hear what they have to say.
Certainly it isn't possible
to cause us to change our way.

WHAT LIES AHEAD?

What lies ahead for us in Life?
Nature can provide some clues.
An interesting statement can be found
in a book that not many use.

It traces the pattern of nature;
nothing simplistic in that way.
Tree leaves blossom each Spring--
then grow, wither, die and decay.

Is that the ultimate end of life?
Of course not! We know that, when
the tree experiences renewal,
its leaves will blossom again.

So what about HUMAN nature?
Is anything simplistic there?
Planted – we bloom, grow and wither;
and death and decay are not rare.

But, praise the Lord, we can trust
as we draw each fleeting breath:
if God sustains even nature,
there truly IS Life after Death!

VIGIL

We watched your face
        for death had robbed you
        and our anguished hearts that wanted so
        to share your pain,
        yet really could not,
        had to settle for the meager pittance
        of our own.

We watched your face
        for signs of your defeat-
        that all the
        sparkling crystals
        of your faith were dulled and
        cast away from you in
        passionate despair.

We watched your face
        and suffered in the wait
        quite twisted with our selfish fears that
        where you led us we were wont
        to go.

We watched your face
        and saw you smile
        through tears once poised and then
        released.
        That smile of sweetness toward
        the thief
        could only spring from
        love complete.

We watched your face
and knew "Christ lives",
and all the self-inflicted wounds of
living
were relieved --
our spirits soared!

WINDOW OF MY LIFE

In never-ending disarray–
broken, stained, the pieces lay.

Useless, wasted was my soul
until I offered God control.

Then, gathering slowly, bit by bit,
He made the jagged pieces fit.

Fused them with His love and grace,
forged for them a resting place.

Fashioned out of pain and strife,
a stained-glass window of my life.

He took the old and made it new
and let His light come shining through.

Love

BOTTOM LINE

Christians are not perfect,
    nor do they look for praise–
they're just ordinary humans
    who've seen the error of their ways.

However, "looking unto Jesus"
    is more than just a whim;
they want to be quite certain
    their eyes are fixed on Him.

They need a steady diet
    of the Holy Spirit's "fruits"
and really must establish
    daily contact with their roots.

The branch can only blossom
    when connected to the Vine,
and Christian lives must demonstrate–
    love is the bottom line.

"HANG-UP"

I understand the basic concept
  of a Christ-like loving Way,
but I have this minor hang-up–
  don't insist that I obey.

I appreciate the ethics
  and believe they're here to stay.
Christian values are important–
  just don't ask me to obey.

I enjoy the cultural trappings
  for the benefits outweigh
any minor maladjustments–
  but don't expect me to obey.

Yet the Scriptures keep repeating
  that our God would hold full sway,
and that Jesus' life is mirrored
  in a single word–"Obey!"

So, Lord, take away my hang-up;
  I would like to try YOUR Way.
We both know it won't be easy,
  but please teach me to obey.

ONE FAITH; ONE BODY

Will we ever come together before our Father's throne?
Or must we keep insisting earthly power's our very own?

Just as mortal bodies need the many parts they're given
So should our Father's Kingdom exist this side of Heaven.

No one body part is stronger and thus must work with others.
all with different functions – yet in sync with one another's

Isn't it amazing each feels they're the one that's right
instead of harmonizing to bring our God delight?

God has plans for all of us; we all have different gifts-
none of them intended to cause so many rifts.

There's just one faith embodied in Jesus Christ, His Son,
and there's no doubt His Spirit must inhabit everyone.

So forgive us, Lord, we pray Thee, whenever we are tempted
to force controlling edicts from which we'd like to be exempted.

Remind us you have spoken through your awesome Word
to make of us One Body - One Faith with one accord.

FEAR

Fear is a paralyzing thing,
controlling us as though a string

Were fastened to our every limb.
Thus, commandeering every whim

Or hope one ever hopes to crave,
the master, FEAR, subdues the slave.

But fat and flabby with success,
ignores the spark of nobleness

Kindled by LOVE–'twill ably crush
the chains of bondage. Then a hush

Will fall on fearful hearts again,
revealing brave, undaunted men.

WEDDING VOWS

It all seems very simple–
a bride walks down the aisle
to a groom who's waiting there
with a sweet and loving smile.

They hold each other's hands
to recite a wedding vow,
and there isn't any doubt,
they mean it here and now.

For better or for worse,
in sickness and in health,
they promise to be faithful
in poverty or wealth.

But a wedding is a pleasure
and, at first, the marriage, too,
but that brand-new way of living
can create a different view.

They may look at one another
and sense a present danger:
"Whatever was I thinking?
I'm married to a stranger!"

Those vows they took together
can shrink and fade away
until they learn the secret
of living day to day.

And place their own reliance
on the Savior's loving ways,
realizing "give" means more than "get"
in the sometimes troubling maze.

Marriage is more than 50/50–
both must give their all
and work to make the other happy,
never building any wall.

Nobody said it would be easy,
but if one wants to make it last;
living and loving together will reflect
those wedding vows from the past.

Looking unto Jesus and trusting
is the only thing to do–
when two hearts really seek Him,
He will surely see them through.

THE JOY OF LOVE

Human love is truly amazing;
there's just one source of true love.
We all have a need for its power
that comes from the Father above.

Love gives a fresh new meaning to life;
giving and forgiving become the norm.
Sacred vows between a husband and wife
ensure a relationship will remain warm.

Love protects, trusts, and renews hope
and, thus, surely will persevere.
with patience and kindness as needed,
it will conquer one's tears and fear.

Love is truly a thing of beauty–
not just some clever ploy.
Whenever its strength remains constant,
lives will be filled with joy.

NIAGARA FALLS

As the "Maid of the Mist" moved slowly
    toward the bottom of the falls,
it looked as though we were heading
    for the center of powerful squalls.

A totally awesome experience–
    to have walls of water all around,
dropping and surging without ceasing
    with great power to astound.

Much later, reflecting on that journey,
    I was reminded of God's great love
powerfully surging all around us,
    cascading without fail from above.

When life's bitter squalls surround us,
    and we are desperately seeking His care,
We definitely must remember
    His great love is there–everywhere!

A LOVING MOTHER'S PRAYER

O, God,

I can help to feed and clothe them,
I can nurse them when they're ill,
I can listen to their troubles,
or mop up a messy spill.

But there is a certain limit
to the aid that I can lend,
and when my service falters,
they will surely need a friend.

So, my mother's prayer is simple:
Once they've departed my command
and are weary and downtrodden,
let them grasp your outstretched hand.

MAN IN THE MOON

A little child perched
on a small church wall
staring in awe at the sky.

Her young eyes were fixed
on a very full moon
without understanding why.

She heard that a man
lived up on that moon;
she thought that sounded queer.

Then, suddenly, it seemed,
a face loomed large-
filling her heart with fear.

I was that small child;
I'm no longer afraid
of my nemesis at night.

The man in the moon
no longer exists;
that fancy has taken flight.

I'm a bit wiser now;
my eyesight is clearly
relieved of my childish fear.

It's just a barren sphere
quite distant from earth
but – when harvest time is here,

It is transformed at night-
an incredible sight,
but its radiance is not its own.

The moon just reflects
the Sun's shining rays
with joy that now is fullblown.

The same way God's Son
brings joy to our hearts-
His love is truly a boon.

Heavenly Father, I pray,
may I reflect His light-
Make my life a true Harvest Moon!

Life

LAMPLIGHTING

A life is an oil lamp that can burn very bright,
filling its spot with a circle of light.

Now, the wick must be trimmed and oil added, one learns.
Thus, each has a hand in the way his lamp burns.

But, in spite of neglect and a glow that grows dim,
God never will quench one that's lifted to Him.

IDOLS

Human hearts
have always longed for
IDOLS
to bow before in
manic adoration.

As long as they are
products of our own making
without obedience or obligation,
we can manipulate the scene.
The form? It matters not–
treasures, celebrities,
entertainment or
lifeless tools of self-indulgence–
seldom do we realize that
what we have created
is never really worthy of our
worship.

Even though that naked truth
may scratch our consciousness,
we eagerly pledge our very lives to the
Idol of the moment.

Oh, living Lord, forgive us all!

69

THE EXILE OF SANITY

Sanity has fled the scene,
      gathering up her skirts
as a gracious, royal queen,
      covering up the hurts.

Brother Reason had been slain
      on the battlefield.
Poor young Logic died in vain–
      wholly unrevealed.

She, seeming very cool and calm,
      feelings held in check,
glossing over icy qualm,
      began her lonely trek

Into exile once again
      to quietly await
her recall by desperate men
      at a later date.

THE TONGUE

The tongue–a human gift quite rare–
can have so many uses.
It can produce a blessing fair
or choose to heap abuses.

A wondrous means to praise the Lord,
to honor Christ His Son–
respect for God's own Living Word
in every spoken one.

It can share a lot of joy with more
and help them to survive;
bring them right to heaven's door
and keep their hopes alive.

But other choices sometimes rule
even well intentioned hearts–
the tongue becomes a weapon cruel
and delivers stinging smarts!

Attempted so-called "humor"
or "sharing" gossip, too,
–what may be just a rumor–
hurts more than just a few.

And when vulgarity begins to flow–
such tawdry, tasteless fare–
the tongue achieves a deeper low
than anyone should dare.

Lord, make us conscious of our flaws,
fill our spirits with your song,
for if we hope to serve your cause,
we must include "the tongue."

THE UNSPOKEN WORD

Most of us do enjoy talking–
    a talent we prove every day.
The words just flow without effort–
    it's normal–what more can I say?

Now, when you are doing the talking,
    you cannot be listening, too,
and God's gift of hearing is wasted
    while we "give the devil his due!"

God gave us two ears for listening,
    and we should make good use of them;
in this wonderful land of the living,
    they are "the crème de la crème."

The question remains: "Which speaks louder"–
    the flurry of sounds in the air
or the unspoken words in our living
    which God finds increasingly rare?

IT'S ALL ABOUT TRUST

My life is filled with staining rust–
Please teach my sinful heart to trust.

I know your cause is truly just–
So lead my selfish heart to trust.

When doubts derail my forward thrust–
Persuade my rebel heart to trust.

Lord, test me if indeed you must–
But grant my anxious heart true trust.

I know I shall return to dust–
First, teach my mortal heart to trust.

A LUKEWARM PRAYER

There is a fear that lingers
with the power to deform,
to find, in time of testing,
a faith that is lukewarm.

When angry winds will buffet
and fierce will rage the storm;
to learn, in painful anguish,
my hope is just lukewarm.

To be rendered ineffectual
by my efforts to conform
to those shadows without pity
with love that's grown lukewarm.

Lord, emptiness consumes me–
fill my spirit with your Form,
let Perfect Love cast out the fear
of being found "lukewarm."

LADDER OF LIFE

My foot slipped a rung on the ladder;
    seems I'll never get to the top.
The ascent is so long and arduous
    while the descent is quick–non-stop.

Sometimes, somewhere near the middle
    when my pace is gradually slowing,
I pause and, just for the moment,
    forget if I'm coming or going.

But, then, in a fresh burst of vigor,
    I press upward, on toward the crown–
I know I can conquer the ladder
    as long as I look UP, not DOWN.

FLAME OF FAITH

Lord, fan the flame of faith so deep within my weary soul.
Grant your mercy with the grace that truly makes me whole,

Crush anger, lust, and vanity that rule my life with ease
while exercising earthly power to bring me to my knees.

As for my Hedonistic longing for passion, power, and pleasure,
replace it with Christ's saving love, which has no earthly measure.

Release me from lip service that would substitute for praise,
and let my daily living reflect His loving ways.

ALL IS WELL

I lived with fear; its acrid smell
encircled with a frightful spell.
God wrapped His hands around my heart–
now, all is well.

I dealt with anger, and its swell
reduced me to a withered shell.
God wrapped His hands around my heart–
now, all is well.

Pain turned on me; it would compel
my life without a parallel.
God wrapped His hands around my heart–
now, all is well.

Grief consumed me, depression fell;
all purpose in life I would repel.
God wrapped His hands around my heart–
now, all is well.

Guilt conquered me–in its prison cell
I suffered more than tongue can tell.
God wrapped His hands around my heart–
now, all is well.

I praise you, God, that naught can quell
my joyful heart's resounding bell.
Your hands are wrapped around my heart–
and ALL is well!

Light

THE POWER OF LIGHT

What is the purpose and power of Light?
It drives away all the Darkness of night.

Light erases the old and life becomes new.
Its merits are many–to cite just a few:

We really need the Light every day
or we cannot see and will lose our way.

Days would then become quite drab and drear
and life's true colors would soon disappear.

Darkness can stunt one's ability to grow
unless it's redeemed in Light's ardent glow.

In darkness, Hope wilts, but when Light is near
hope can be healed and will drive away fear.

Light has the Power to warm hands and heart
and gives one the courage to make a fresh start.

There really is only one True Source of Light–
our Father in Heaven whose love sets us right.

His Light is available to everyone
who flees the Darkness and follows His Son.

A RAINBOW IS A PROMISE

Look–over there! It's a rainbow
arching its way through the sky,
replacing a host of dark storm clouds
determined to terrify.

The cloudburst has suddenly ended
though fierce was its raging despair,
and bitter the brew for the moment
that had boiled in the angry air.

But fear dissipates; hope awakens
and soars to a dizzying height.
Terror dispelled by a vision–truth
wrought in the splendor of Light.

This dazzling display of color
is a heavenly visual aid,
for a rainbow reflects a promise–
the love of God never will fade.

TUNNELS OF LIFE

Entering a "tunnel of life," I saw
        the way was dimly lit.
I could not change direction
        and knew I couldn't quit.

As I traveled through the tunnel,
        it seemed I had no choice.
The way was long and dreary–
        then I heard a still small Voice.

"Do not be discouraged, child,
        there's light at the tunnel's end.
My Son will share your journey
        and will surely be your friend."

The dreariness was drained away
        and great light filled the place,
for even in life's tunnels, we
        can know God's wondrous grace.

PARALYZING FOG

A misty blanket of fog
envelops the earth–
a cloudlike mass
obscures the light and
darkness rules.

Those entrapped within
that darkened atmosphere–
      bewildered
            perplexed
                  confused
and sadly unaware
that True Light does exist–
become
a nation of fools.

O, beloved country,
seek the Light before it is
too late!

Eternity

THE FORCE OF EVIL

The force of evil is unrestrained–
it permeates a way of life as
    entertainment,
    freedom speech,
    civil liberty, and
    human license in many forms.

Resistance would be easier perhaps
if evil wore an evil look.
But much too clever for such simplicity,
preferring fanciful facades,
it whispers promises of
warm and lovely pleasures
or just entitlement–
pure and without pain.

Its dangers and delights do
cloud the minds of those
indulging freely
while ridiculing the ones
who choose another path.

Evil gives no quarter–
its relentless imposition will impair
the best of judgment
and lend no pity
to consequences borne of
so-called freedom that
often does deny
the same to others.

It nibbles at a
nation's heart and soul
and then
devours the whole.

NIGHT MUSIC

Ah, the alluring
music of the night with its
beauty and power
to entice, to mesmerize,
and captivate my thinking;
thus, surrounding my life with
pleasure beyond measure.

But it delights in evil and
offers only darkness
imprisoning those
within its cold embrace.

Flee! O flee, my soul!
Pursue the ever present
glimmer of eternal light
that offers hope and joy and
freedom from the ultimate
misery of darkness!

HERE AND NOW

If a miracle should happen
    right here–right now
in the middle of a day well ordered,
    would I notice?

If an angel spoke to me
    right here–right now
in the din of daily living,
    would I hear?

If Love reached out to me
    right here–right now
In the depths of desperate longing,
    would I respond?

THE SEED OF FAITH

I struggle for meaning
with man-made tools–
    logic
    reason
    determination
    discipline
    industry
earnestly believing
they are inextricably involved with
    success
    comfort
    contentment
    condition of life.

But it never all comes together
and I find myself
    lonely
    frustrated
    bored
    pursuing escape in sundry form,
straining at the seams and
fearing
it will all come apart.

I reach
in desperation
into the seeming distant past
and seize upon a
kernel of faith
long ago discarded as
    impractical
    illogical
    unreasonable,
discovering in delight
it only needed a chance to grow.

I make a monumental decision–
I kneel, plant, and water
the seed of faith.

THE WRONG SIDE

Standing at the iron gate
      with a wistful glance,
the garden was so beautiful
      with its power to entrance.

I gazed between the heavy bars
      at heaven's scenery
and realized very sadly that
      I didn't have a key.

If only I had heeded
      Jesus' loving, patient call;
instead I wanted my own way,
      and for this I gave my all.

I recall the key Christ offered,
      but now it is too late.
So here I stand with broken heart
      on the wrong side of the gate.

COMING AND GOING

How do I get from here to there?
How do you get from here to where?
Perhaps you've never been made aware;
Surely it isn't that you don't care.

First, you must choose a way to go –
Any old way won't do, you know.
Many a way is a way of woe,
So strive for the highest – not the low.

If that is your preference, here is good news.
There is a Way which all can choose
and if it's followed, no one can lose.
Wouldn't you wonder why any refuse?

"I AM THE WAY" of real living, said He.
None comes to the Father, except by me.
Then, proving His promise, He paid the fee.
That's how the WAY began to be.

The WAY's not an easy journey at all.
So remember if you should heed His call-
as you travel His path, you must stand tall
and, tho you may stumble, He won't let you fall.

We come and we go, often deep in despair,
believing our own situation is rare.
Spend just a moment kneeling in prayer-
that's how you get from here to there!

SUNSETS

Sunset signals the end of day
but not until the final ray
has totally been drained away.

What will replace that sky of blue
when the sun slides slowly out of view?
Will all that's old become brand new?

Will the sun still shine and be really clear,
bathing all in gold as the end draws near?
Will love completely cast out fear?

Will clouds obscure life as the sun grows cold
and darken our hopes as death's drums are rolled,
or will they enhance what our eyes behold?

Those colors that linger when the sun has fled,
the crimson, the purple, the orange, and the red–
will they fade forever–leaving what instead?

What will that sunset be like for me?
Will it an end or beginning be?
There is no way mortal eyes can see.

It matters not how I fume and fret;
one thing is certain–the sun will set–
but with eyes of faith my needs will be met.

I can only trust in God's mercy and grace,
believe in His promises and seek His dear face,
knowing He's prepared a far better place.

Gloria Yoder Ewachiw

Gloria Ewachiw began writing Christian poetry when her three children were preschoolers. A busy mother, she discovered writing as not only an inexpensive hobby requiring only pencil and paper but also an escape into a personal, quiet world.

In time, her writing expanded into preparing dramas for Sunday School classes, programs for women's Christian retreats, and scripts for stewardship campaigns. Now retired, Gloria has added newsletter articles and variety shows to her repertoire.

To her, writing is a treasured, lifelong friend with "whom" she can be happy or sad, humorous or cantankerous as she writes to express her faith and demonstrate her convictions.